WHERE ZEBRAS GO

In memory of Dad, who first gave me poetry, for Mum and her rhyming bones, Mark, who encouraged me and Danny, Tasha and Holly, without whom my rhymes would have no reason.

Text and illustrations copyright © Sue Hardy-Dawson 2017 except for:
A Question of a Snake copyright © 2005, *The Frog Princess* copyright © 2009, *Holiday Blues* copyright © 2009, *The Kiss* copyright © 2013, *Old Dog* copyright © 2011, *Old Foxy* copyright © 2012, *Planet for Sale* copyright © 2008, *Poem about the Injustice of Being Made to Stand Outside in the Rain at Playtime* copyright © 2009, *The Poe Tree* copyright © 2011, *Talking Toads* copyright © 2010, *Terrible Lizards* copyright © 2009, *Where Zebras Go* copyright © 2014

First published in Great Britain and in the USA in 2017 by
Otter-Barry Books
Little Orchard, Burley Gate, Hereford, HR1 3QS

www.otterbarrybooks.com

A catalogue record for this book is available from the British Library.

ISBN 978-1-91095-931-2

Illustrated with mixed media

Printed in Great Britain by Martins the Printers

1 3 5 7 9 8 6 4 2

WHERE ZEBRAS GO

Poems and Illustrations by
Sue Hardy-Dawson

Otter-Barry BOOKS

CONTENTS

7

THE WEAVER OF WORDS

Wind, rattles clouds
carrying the song
of the weaver of words.
Coarse-fingered
nails, polished
to the points of needles.

She winds *Dazzling*
from skeins of sunlight.
Skilfully she weaves
from an ape's fist,
Deceit from a spider's tears,
Deftly her fingers dance.
Azure, Cornflower
float towards the sky.

Catching threads
she joins consonants to vowels
whispers them to the wind
and out into the waking world.

9

GREY GHOSTS

We   are   more
precious **than ivory. Listen**, and
you will he**ar us walking,** under trees,
in the tra**cery of evening.** Look for our
empty sh**adows at** da**wn,** far beyond su**n**
light now **reaching, acro**ss another dream
pale sav**annah, grieving** kinship, **we have**
mour**ned, with our** dead's **exquisite**
m**a**r**quetry. Of our bones,** each
once breathed, felt **all, the**
dry heat days and dark-
ness in the **moon times,**
we who have   **loved**
and are loved. **Behind**
 each cold tusk,   feel
our still eyes staring
back **at you, for we are**
the **true cost. Remember us.**

FOG WARNING

Today sky will be heavy in all places
and some streets may be without colour.

Dew could develop later in hedges
whilst telegraph wires will hang about unseen.

Grey trees will smoulder darkly
and there are strong warnings of muted grass.

It's likely houses may seem patchy.
Expect most riverbanks to appear faded
with high probabilities of willows weeping.

Flowers are advised not to open unless they must
as misty sunlight will tend to be fleeting.

Generally birdsong is going to be hushed
giving little chance for a glimpse of its furtive singers.

Everywhere cobwebs will drip chandeliers.

WHERE ZEBRAS GO

where the amber river slows
where the alligator wallows
where the cruel acacia grows
where the hippo haunts the shallows

where the sleeping lions doze
where antelope meekly swallow
where the sky and land sit close
where the trees are dark as gallows

where the hot wind ebbs and flows
where the grass is coarse and fallow
where the plains grow dry as bones
where the earth is scorched and yellow

where the desert soil corrodes
where the trees are parched and sallow
where vultures stoop, in funeral clothes
where the clouds are looming shadows

Sirocco or *Scirocco* is a Mediterranean wind that comes from the Sahara,
reaching hurricane speeds in North Africa, bringing the rains.

where the dust creeps down the road
where the air is still and hollow
where mountains fall and woodlands close
where the mud is thick as tallow

where the elephants leave their bones
where gazelle and bison follow
where the great Sirocco blows
where the rains go – zebra goes

WHEN I WAS FAMOUS

For a while
when I was small
I was famous.
Friends and relatives
queued to see
tiny me.

My first words
so profound
I was called on
to repeat them
and I'm told
that I performed
brilliantly.

My crawling
caused applause
I remember
reported down the phone
to every family member.
How could I know
that it would end
when I stopped being little?
But fame, it seems
is rather fickle.

OLD FOXY

The
urban
fox waits for Monday night's
feast, of Sunday's roast chicken bones,
jellied and greased. Lunch in
the lamplight. Fish heads
with leeks, crisp
rinds of
bacon
and pizza
midweek.
Brave bin
buccaneer,
midnight's
dark thief, of
pittas with curry,
smoked ham or
corned beef. So
while the house
dozes and Heel-
Nipper sleeps, Old
Foxy hunts hedges
then craftily creeps
up on packed lunches,
down wild city streets,
for the cold fatty flavours
of half-eaten treats.
Then
with
sliced
mutton
sliver and
sausage for
sweet, slinks
back in the
shadows, to
his grand
country
seat.

NO ARGUMENT

Below is the best poem I've ever written.
It alliterates attractively,
has imagery that illuminates the page,
metaphors that melt in the mouth,
its similes shimmer like star dust
and its perfect punctuation pauses it,

in all the right places...

Unfortunately I wrote it in invisible ink,
but it's dead good. Honest!

MOLE

A fine gentleman in his black moleskin
though his jet eyes have long sunk, pin-like

and his homely tomb requires no pit-lamp
to shift his affairs, or shuffle dirt backwards.

He desires no prop-shaft to empty out casts
or turn somersault on his slagheap doorstep.

Old shovel-hands picking seams, sickle-thumbed
in pink leather gauntlets, folding up the earth.

A grab-faced miner of rich worm fissures
he's soil's dark drab, digging pallid root girders.

Working undercover at mud's belly, stone
ribs; loamy flesh for his soporific larder.

Sunless, moonless, he wakes, sleeps, beneath
dust skies, bulb clouds, bedded in earth's womb

of grass and leaf, whiskery, feely, he's spent
keeping his skin his own, dark, in a lone burrow.

POETRY OLYMPICS RULES

1 Please remember Hai
ku jump should never exceed
seventeen syllab...

2 No sticks in L'acrostics.

3 Enormous leaps of imagination are discouraged
in the Epitaphalon.

4 All teams must go up as well as down in the
palindrome.

5 All teams should wear their poetry kit
and keep their muses under control at all times.

6 Only Sumo-perlatives may carry a hot water
bottle.

7 Couplets are eligible for Ode style dancing.

8 Crashing and clanging are fine, but kayaking
and canoeing are banned
from the Onomatopoeia.
Note: no Ballads allowed to keep boats upright.

9 Warning: those kenning late may not finish.

10 Those kenning early may not be able to get in.
All stressed syllables are entitled to counselling.
   Discuss…

NOTE those caught alliterating are likely to face fierce
fines and Free Verse doesn't mean you don't have to pay
to get in.

*Historically, the Olympic Games was a religious festival
including, not just sport, but competitions for poets and
sculptors.*

LICODIMA LEOPARD

Likodima
leopard,
mistress   of
disguise, midnight
and   moon   light
fill   her   empty
eyes. Dancing in   the
grasses,   the
ghost   of   her
embrace,   Licodima,
no   one   sees
her,   taken

by   surprise.

Licodima
leopard,
with her
coat
of
stars,
in blackened
constellations   of   ashen
battle   scars. Hiding

in   the   tree
top,   above   the
arid   plains,

Licodima, no   one
sees   her,   or

her
children
starve.

Licodima
leopard,   dark   against
the sky,   mid night   and   moon   light watch the slow sun rise,
folded   in   the   branches,   the   shadows   of   her eyes.
Licodima,   just a   dreamer,   wishing
she   could   fly.

WHO

I'm a shadow, feathered glider
a velvet-winged deep-sky-diver
a lightning strike, storm-blown twister
a spiky, sweet meadow-drifter.

I'm the moon's soft shape-shifter
the iced bite of starlit winter, death's
colder, harder, bitter sister, the dark cloud
rider and great bone grinder.

I am midnight's pale squatter, Earth's
sudden bomb-dropper, a dark mine-sweeper
the rude rodent-stealer of dim moonless
hollows and edges of burrows.

RISING EARLY

The cold is solid,
hard against thighs,
steel to toe.
In the mirror of the gas fire
my face distorts,
thin, too long.

We giggle,
push to hog the heat,
burning knees
freeze at the sides.
We struggle into steaming clothes,
nudge and pinch.

As the sky lightens
through the kitchen window
mist trails up the track,
sun struggles over banks
pooled with frost-burnt clouds.

We pull on icy socks,
itchy vests,
their labels brittle.

Red-cheeked, slump-eyed,
we bite and snap hot porridge,
drip down scalding toast,
pull on stiff gloves and coats.
Then, spilling out our misty breaths,
we rattle booted down the path.

GUILTY AS CHARGED

I'm very guilty
very, very guilty
guilty of a crime
I've never heard of.

I didn't know it.
Imagine, not knowing it.
I didn't *know better*
unfortunately.

Mum said I should've.
Dad agreed with her.
I wish that I'd known it
but I just didn't see.

When I asked them
please explain it
they both got really angry,
said, *if you don't know now
you never ever will!*

It's really kind of sad
and very disappointing
to know that
I will never
know better
now!

HOW TO SCORE A PENALTY

Wearing Grandad's
boots, that scored the winner
back in fifty-two; always tie the left
boot first, then   insist on waiting
till the moon is   full. Sprinkle the
pitch with four
leafed clover,
  bury a sixpence
    under a stile, wish
      on a star, consult the
          heavens, promise a
            witch your first-born
              child. Check your
horseshoe's   right side up, swear
an oath on a   loved one's grave.
Though tricky,   dragon's teeth are
handy for   stopping goals
from being   saved. Buy
  a talisman from a   friendly wizard,
    avoid black cats   and poisoned roots,
      lastly, test the wind direction, but HOOT!
        never close your eyes, then

28

M**UT**E

Sitting in the centre of the pitch
waiting for the first foot
the ball holds its breath
eyes raised we all
watch the coin fall
slap – whistle – thud
someone turns up the crowd.

TALKING TOADS

Oh it's so mean to talk of his bumptious warts, as rather rough and too grubbily. And please don't squeal, if he offers a meal that's sort of wriggly, struggly. Don't stare if he lurks, with lubricious jerks or stiffly sniffs around muddily. And if he's not slim, lacking much of a chin, his tongue is so gorgeously bubbly. A rainbow disguise would be lacking surprise in his insecticidal thuggery. No sepia skin and gargantuan grins suit all manner of clammier muggery. Whilst his slippery state attracts murksome mates, who are scrumptiously slimy and stubbly. What if these perfections are sour reflections of homes mostly rankish and rubbly. So languorously lank, full of simmering swank, he grazes the slack and the slovenly. Gorgeously guileless, stupendously stylish, yet so very deliciously ugly.

FIRE ESCAPE

The grate was empty.
Outside the smell
of wood smoke lingers.

Coal prints across the lawn.

DRAGON SONG

Where the darkness meets the moon
there's a cast of angry light
over treetops
in the gloom
drifts the hint of burning eyes.

Weary as a mountain weeping
swallowing the hush of night
floating silent
wings unseen
shadows creep and fire flies.

Whispering the frosty air
far above the bitter ice
out beyond
dark careless stars
dragon tastes the wind and sighs.

Worn away to shades of dust
soaring over cool starlight
fly his ghostly
dragon brothers
from the clouds he softly cries.

Where the morning slowly creeps
past the waning of the night
into shadows
falling mists
dragon creeps away and hides.

Sleeping in his boiling layer
bathed in sulphur, glowing bright
dragon dreams
his dragon brothers
carry him through ancient skies.

MERMAID

My song is silence, wind
and wave, I salt grave
sailed gulls, grind
my ire
on
callous cliffs, flimsy ships.
I'm spray-washed squall,
dropped carrion's mist,
I rot
mute
sleepers in mussels' fists, dust
dark weeds, musty seeds.
In constant deep
I ebb
and
flow. And as I go, I'm one with
slow, gilt shoals, long
fluttering tides, a
coif of
clay.
I tremble, sway, sing and coil
surf and sand until the land's
gusted dunes are
silent
shrouds.

My song is bitter, bile, oyster
silver's hidden pearl. Long
eyed, he smiled.
I loved
him
once, was nothing loth to
sell my soul, for feet of ice
and a silent song.

UGLY SISTER SONNET

Born plain, we pinch to watch her blue eyes fill,
Buy a cat to kill the mice that she adores.
Her trousseau and her mother's clothes we steal,
Tear apart her exotic hand-sewn clothes.
We loathe the pretty birds that comb her hair
And sickly sweetness, just like beauty, palls.
The sunlight in her smile must bring despair
And tuneful singing soon begins to bore.
Yet we're still haunted by her wistful gaze,
We're jealous of her peace and innocence,
The girl who won't take task or disobey,
Or as in past behaviour take offence.
So we all wait but no prince comes to call.
She, weeping in the grate, we at the ball.

LEGEND

The rat's as sharp as a spinning needle
to speak his name will cast a spell
the seventh child of seven brothers
he hears the wishing
of the well

he seeks glass slippers among the cinders
the darkest wood contains a feast
and though he possesses such rare beauty
to some he is a
fearsome beast

far more resourceful than any feline
his boots are made from dragon scale
and even though a flute once tamed him
he's still the stuff
of furry tails.

THE FROG PRINCESS

Well
OK Dad, it was
something like this.   At
first I found him slimy   and
I regret, wet. I know of course   looks aren't
everything, I'm just not really sure   about green. So
what if he did find my golden ball, I didn't   once mention
a kiss. More like I put him gently over the wall. Oh well
then – maybe, as you suggest, it was the teeniest little
kick. Then naturally, I ran and ran, as only really a true
princess can, in silly shoes and a dress. I never once
dreamed that he would follow – No, Dad,   stop
        don't   say a word. Imagine this, he
        wanted   to sleep on my pillow, to
eat off the very   same plate. It really
isn't   hygienic, a point
                    I tried but failed
                    to make. Well
                    at any rate, I
                    saw a flash
                    and all at
                    once he was
                    such a dreamy date.
                    So we live in a pond,
                        where he is king.
                            The children
                                will hatch
                                in early spring.
                            Yes, it seems
                        love changes
                    everything.

SNOW GREY

No one wished for her
an unhappy surprise.
Ebony teeth, she's sour thin,
eyes dull as slush.
No man, bird or beast
flocked to her song.

One only a mother could love.
But she did not. Once, kicked
from the house of seven trolls,
she fixes her smile and sighs
for a prince's child.

A pretty witch spies
her eating flies,
gets her to close eight eyes,
makes her sweet.
Then, wrapped in stars,
she finds her prince
and after a kiss – devours him.

THE PIED PIPER'S WIFE

No, not the first strange thing
he'd brought back.
Unicorns, rare even then,
flocks of dragons
and skulks of red foxes,
grey mountain wolves,

whole forest trees
and, just once,
a Pharaoh's sores.
But mostly locusts, toads,
bats and cats.
Worse, when he brought back
fat, black rats,
a sea captain's ghostly pirate band.

Me? I liked the children best,
sweet, if a little faded,
though I tried to tell him
I only wanted one, two at most.

Full of pride, he'd not let go.
The pipes had changed them,
sleepwalking in a half world,
children that won't grow,
following him wherever he goes
climbing, trees, mountains,
looking for reasons,
dark dreams, songs of spun gold.

TWENTY WAYS TO AVOID MONSTERS AND MYTHICAL BEASTS

1 If your granny has a long thin furry face, consider the following: a) she's a werewolf. b) she's the big bad wolf. Either way, see a woodcutter before visiting her and under no circumstances comment on the size of her teeth.

2 Don't climb anything that grew taller than a house in one night.

3 Don't make bargains that include your first-born child.

4 Don't eat buildings made of gingerbread.

5 Don't talk to witches, but take care to ignore them politely.

6 Don't play in caves unless you paid to get in.

7 If you do, avoid large eggs that smell of pumice.

8 If you find a trolls' nest don't dig up their gold.

9 Don't stand and howl at the moon.

10 If you hear noises in the middle of a wood, don't investigate them.

11 Don't check under the bed or in cupboards: get some other sucker to do it.

12 Never buy anything that has the first name *Magic* or *Gigantic*.

13 If your name is *Beauty* make it clear you hate roses, unless they've come from a shop.

14 Avoid women with green snaky hair. Only look at them in mirrors.

15 If anything with too many legs, arms, eyes or heads speaks to you, ignore it.

16 If anyone, apart from your parents, tells you they're gonna eat you up, believe them.

17 If your parents have a distant look about them (look up Zombies and Alien Possession) believe them too.

18 Don't hug anything hairy with rotten table-manners, unless it's your dad.

19 Wrap yourself in cotton wool.

20 Wear deodorant, to stop them smelling your fear.

NOTE NO RESPONSIBILITY WILL BE TAKEN FOR ANYONE WHO IGNORES THIS NOTICE.

P.S. Always wear a coat over your cotton wool or you might attract the wrong kind of attention.

THE BOX

She had a box full of taffeta, ermine,
shoes made of petals, those of a rose.
Satin, worn thin beneath copper trees,
a deep scarlet hood on a wolfish coat.

She had a shadowy wizard's curtain,
a diamond tiara, cold giant's gold,
spider silk scarves, spun in the breeze,
the Queen of Persia's purple robes.

She had a pipe for charming vermin,
the enchanted horn from a unicorn,
a princess's quilt, a bag of dry peas,
precious stones, a gift from the trolls.

She had a ring, made in a mountain,
a splinter of oak from an elfish boat,
a swan's crown made of silver leaves,
bricks made of straw, long flaxen ropes.

She had a ball from a crystal fountain,
shards with a mote, from a mirror that spoke,
a puppet's long nose, a harp that weeps,
a needle that pricks, a witch's warm cloak.

All this she showed me, of this I'm certain,
her magical box, the tales that she told.
Forbidden to touch them, one day I stole
its ebony key and some beans which I sold....

WOLF

As the muffled evening settles
moonlight pours across the floor
something in the shadows flickers
instinct lifts his grizzled jaw.

Gazing at the cloudless heavens
he sings the notes of distant stars
the songs his fathers have forgotten
beyond a world of streets and cars.

Lilting notes of coursing rivers
mournful cries on empty moors
steaming footfalls in the darkness
the garden wolf is tame no more.

Daylight often finds him yawning
or softly padding across the floor
tenderly he'll rise to greet you
then whimper by the kitchen door.

SHAGGY DOG STORY

Er,   I
did   do my
homework Miss, but er ...
my homework ate my
dog! So we had to call
a policeman
to catch and
tell it off. But
it wouldn't come
quietly, so we locked it in
the loo, and called a homework
hunter, to ask him what to do. He set
a great big homework trap, which took
till   half-past ten, he made it spit our dog
out   and   told them   to make friends.
But   my home   work, it's   still
sulking   Miss,   and   will
not come   to school,   I've   told it
that   I'm for it   and it's   broken
every   rule. No   Miss,   I know
Miss but   you must   believe   it's true.
I know   it sounds   ridiculous   but I'd
never   lie to   you.

CITY DOGS

One dog: knows grass is
square, that trees align to
cross the road and litterbins
form sullen packs. He stalks
dull pavements, greasy paths,
tracks fat cars, drenched with
diesel breath, sniffs parched
moss for straggled weeds or
rats that hover under cracks.

One dog: reads wall, door,
Eau de Cologne of city cats,
does old paw shuffle or long
claw taps, in a Burberry coat
or tartan slacks, down alleys
bright with grey lamplight
he chats by neon *Cosy Caffs*
or under bridges, vacant flats,
sips an oilskin looking-glass.

One dog: guards his patch
of tenements, launderettes,
his *à la carte* refuge sacks
he keeps from mongrels,
country curs, wild beneath
the pylon stacks, grizzled,
raggle-taggle, spare, he spikes
the night with snaps and scraps
calling out for air! Air! Air!

OLD DOG

The cats don't worry any more.
Word's out: five minutes' walk
from bed to chair. This year the
fireworks weren't a pain. You
didn't even seem to hear. Dull-
eyed, head buried in my lap, you
lift my hand, dry-nosed, and I
caress the grey straw of your fur.

You were never beautiful or good,
a raggle-taggle mischief of a dog.
But that was long ago... now
in your dreams you run and play,
and we, who cursed half-eaten shoes,
smile as you sniff secret smells
in a doggy heaven we can't share.

POEM ABOUT THE INJUSTICE OF BEING MADE TO STAND OUTSIDE IN THE RAIN AT BREAK-TIME

It's
not
fair!

SCHOOL HOLIDAY BLUES

From our empty classroom escapes a little sigh,
as if it really misses having children milling by.
Its desktops look so lonely, they smell alien and
clean. The bin is black and sullen, no litter to be
seen. The numbers sit in silence, refusing to add
up, between the mournful pencils and the unread
reading books. Pens
stand to attention,
chairs all wait in line. The only property
is lost. An unwatched clock marks time.
There's only one sad trainer and an empty
pencil case, hanging off the coat pegs; our
hall is just a space
and outside, in the
playground, birds,
with no snacks to
eat, watch an old
grey ball moved **eet.**
along by unseen

CROC

There's really nothing quite so vile
as those who loathe the crocodile.
He's gentle, sweet and rather shy
and truly wouldn't harm a fly.

It can't be helped if current styles
abhor his coat of polished tiles.
No wonder he so often hides
by rubbing mud on all his sides.

It's true, his favourite salad dish
may contain the odd missed fish,
and he's wary of his long thin chin
lest something trip and then fall in.

He can't be blamed, if by mistake
your arms or legs land in his lake.
His guilty tears you may despise
despite his most enchanting eyes.

But those who land on crocodiles
care little for engaging smiles,
and less still for croc's tender tum
as poor digestion makes him glum.

It's kindness that is his undoing –
he knows what hurts is all that chewing.
So stay quite calm for what must follow
and he won't chew you when he swallows.

TERRIBLE LIZARDS

Who says there are no dinosaurs?
Hiding quieter than mice
under fjords of blue ice
waiting for the land to thaw
dreaming of their winter store
ancient dreams they've dreamt before.

Who says there are no dinosaurs?
Lurking darkly in deep pools
slumbering inside green hills
enormous wings and dreadful roar
burning eyes and horns that gore
or trapped beneath the ocean floor.

Who says every dinosaur
died of cold and turned to stone?
Lumbering beast with giant bones
heavy feet and teeth that tore
deathly grip and iron jaw
armoured scales and fearful claw.

Who says every last one died?
Lurking darkly in deep pools
slumbering inside green hills
under fjords of blue ice
waiting for the world to thaw
trapped beneath the ocean floor.

Who says every last one died?
Perhaps some sleep and others hide....

DINING WITH DINOSAURS

If you dare
to dine with dinosaurs
explain it's rude to
eat ⌇⌇⌇⌇⌇⌇⌇⌇⌇
front
doors, ⌇⌇⌇⌇⌇⌇⌇⌇
and if they make holes in
your floors, never
reward
them with applause.
Their tiny brains can hardly think,
so never let them play   with   ink,
and discourage paddling
in the sink or tipping toilets
up to drink. It's hard to stop
them chewing chairs and
damaging the hall and stairs,
importantly, such small repairs
should   never   catch
you unawares.   But if   you
dine   with   dinosaurs,
you   may find   that it's
good   to pause,   and
  before   you let
      them
           all
      indoors
    make
      sure
        that
          they
              are

60

herbivores.

NOVEMBER

Golden flowers bloom in the sky
spreading out lace
till
they
drop
like fireflies
biting the back of my throat
jacket potato fog, a Catherine wheel spits.

Above the sulphured air, sparks die
toffee smoking breath
jumps
out
in shouts
and squeals.
Children skip around the fire's tongues
like mad moths, waving sparkling wands.

Sparklers fizzle, plop into buckets that sigh.
Soup by the trestle-load
raw
kneed
boy scouts
scrawl messy signs
tissue fists of hotdogs glide, steaming
in clouds of onion, coins clink, hats pulled down.

Only the Guy prays for rain. He doesn't know
it always rains.

PENGUIN

On land I'm slow,
flat-footed,
stunted, low,
coarse-voiced
like grit on timber.
A stone-backed
shuffler, shorn
at the neck.
I bounce, I
lumber, coaled,
chalked, to pause
at the batons
of cliff, to
slip its brink,
drip into
iced ocean.

But when I
dive in, swim
in blue-green
silence, where
echoes are
dancers, each
limb is a wing.
I'm half-fish,
half-bird,

a silver-scaled
mermaid of
droplets on
skin, drifting
the surface,
sink deeper
or skim. I'm
floating on
bubbles, green,
willowy,
thin as the
voice of the
waves coming in.

SLUDGE-BOG STEW

I'm a spiky salamander
a dizzy dragon doppelganger
a strutting, sticky super-slammer
a bluebottle and insect hanger.

But down in the swamp where the mud's like glue
we love sludge-bog
pickled frog and sludge-bog
yes, we love sludge-bog
sludge-bog stew!

I'm a slithering, skinny snake
a rude reptilian, wriggling rake
a hissing, haggling, hot headache
if swallowed whole, it's your mistake.

But down in the swamp where the mud's like glue
we love sludge-bog
pickled frog and sludge-bog
yes, we love sludge-bog
sludge-bog stew!

I'm a cranky crocodile
a juddering, jerking juvenile
I'm violent, vain and volatile
to struggle would be quite futile.

But down in the swamp where the mud's like glue
we love sludge-bog
pickled frog and sludge-bog
yes, we love sludge-bog
sludge-bog stew!

I'm a flippy floppy frog
a moping, moaning monologue
an undisputed underdog
and I'm hiding in this muddy bog.

But down in the swamp where the mud's like glue
I hate sludge-bog
pickled aargh! and sludge-bog
yes, I HATE sludge-bog
sludge-bog stew!

MAKING TIGERS

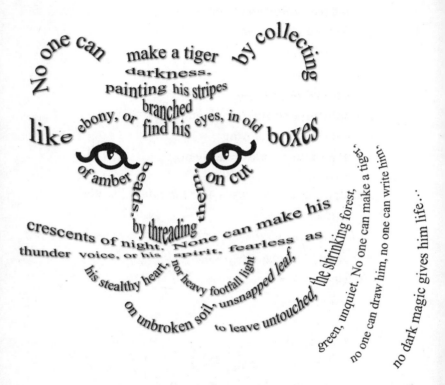

No one can make a tiger by collecting darkness. painting his stripes like ebony, or find his eyes, in old boxes branched of amber beads, on cut crescents of night. None can make his by threading them, thunder voice, or his spirit, fearless as his stealthy heart, nor heavy footfall light on unbroken soil, unsnapped leaf, to leave untouched, the shrinking forest, green, unquiet. No one can make a tiger no one can draw him, no one can write him no dark magic gives him life…

MO**ON** POEM

Here on the moon
we don't chase morning,
we just swim backwards
too high, too slow.

And we can't sail the moon-sea
on ships dreamt by children
sleeping below.

Here on the moon
we don't bounce pebbles,
they'd just spin upwards
too far, too still.

And the cow never jumped here
she just followed the cat
over the hill.

Here on the moon
we don't hear moon-shells,
there's only the silence
too pale, too small.

And we stars search the darkness
to wish on bright people
hoping they will fall.

THE BEAUTIFUL PLANET

Hello, hello, this is Captain Stark
from the starship Campion.
Can we land on your beautiful planet?
Early indications suggest adequate oxygen.
It seems we have detected
all we need to set up home.
But where do you come from, travellers?
Have you no planet of your own?

Yes, we once had a planet
just as beautiful as yours
but the lakes all turned to acid
and the seas drowned out its shores.
Trees and grasses were dying
and the air became dusty and thin.
But why was it dying, travellers?
How did this thing begin?

Gasses from our factories
killed grass and poisoned trees
and as the sun grew hotter
icecaps melted into seas.
Water swallowed up our homes
and made our Earth soggy clay.
Such terrible gasses, travellers,
that they killed a world in one day?

Oh no, it took centuries
to cut down all the trees,
for all the animals to die
from the gas in the factories.
But our leaders just wouldn't listen,
it was a terrible mistake.
But what were factories for,
travellers? What did the factories make?

Wonderful, useful, brilliant things,
marvellous inventions,
bigger, better and faster machines
too helpful and useful to mention.
We couldn't do without them.
No, no one could do without these.
Yet they couldn't make air
and they couldn't make trees?

Hello! Hello! Can you hear me?
Captain Stark - the - star - ship - Campion,
may we land on your beautiful planet?
Please! Please can you help us?
We can't - hold - out - too - long....

THE POE TREE

The Poe tree
is perfect. The   Poe tree
is   likable. It doesn't need
sunlight   and it's   totally
recyclable. You can   cut it into
pieces and stick it   back together.
It isn't spoiled   by acid rain
or washed out by the river. It's a
shame about the other trees,
I was kind   of fond
of   them,
I   think
I'll miss
bright
green
leaves.

and

maybe
oxygen.
But Poe trees
are perfect. Poe trees
are likable. They don't need sunlight and they're totally recyclable.

PLANET FOR SALE

In need of some repair,
six point seven billion
careless owners.
Lovely views of the galaxy,
possible renovation project.

Owners seek exchange
with similar elsewhere
in universe.
Must have sun.
Plenty of money for
a shiny new model
with an ozone layer.

PANDA

High   in the
mountain   forests, I
hide,   the

depths   of an
ocean in   still dark
eyes. Quiet   as a ghost
fish   folding

the rivers,
I pluck green
rattan

with
thumb   and fingers
and sip the clear cold mountain waters,
where banks of cloud join land to sky. I, half
in shadow and half in light, I am neither black
nor yet all white. I am almost a dream of long
ago. I am   snow on dark rocks,
ebony on   snow. Yet I see
all as I slowly   go, among
the leaf   cloaked
wastes of ice.   Half
light, half   shadow
I come and go,   from those who've
claimed my   lands below. And
whilst I fish   or steal an egg or
two, for   most of the time
I slowly chew,   on the high cool
forests of sweet bamboo. And
though I'm   close you'll
never know.

MOON BATHING

We built you with cold hands,
foggy breath, panting as you
grew. Rolled down the hill,
your soft skull glitters in late
sunlight; we pinch your frozen
lips, lace them with coal. Shy

in your stiff new coat, your
young soul's old. A week of
freeze hardens you, black milk
teeth dance around your smile,
stick limbs shiver with delight
as you bask in frosted ice, or

catch moon's silver on long
white lashes. I sense the wink
of sleet in your face – as you
sink. Your feet luxuriate, sharp,
brittle in snow, you seduce stars
with your pale hailstone heart.

You fear their warmth, the air
collides, your head grows slow,
heavy, grey labyrinths of tears
glisten, white scars soften as,
silently, you slip away into the
darkening pools of moonlight.

HARE'S NIGHT SONG

See her moonlight
bloom from thick forest

leaving the ground
plucking words from the stars

half heather mosses
deep purple wherries

strains of midnight shadow
rise from the earth

she reads diamond notes
on silver grasses

from black glassy brooks
damp reedy lairs

leaving her thin voice
where darkness passes

in the ghost of her
limpid, lamplight
stare

CHRISTMAS ANGEL

*

In
the
dark the
Christmas
angel dreams
a tinsel spangled
sleep Of children
waiting, faces glowing,
underneath the scented
tree . She sighS amOngst
the paper lanterns, muddled in
their nest Of starS. Wakes tO the
mOonbeams sOftly singing, silver
glitters in the dark. FrOst danCes in
the empty garden until the SnOw
begins to fall. SoOn she thinks, when
night
draws
in and below
the eaves the
children call.

THE COLOUR OF MOONLIGHT

Moonlight's a summer shadow
a smile at the edge of the moon
a blanket to hang the stars from
a mask for a lover's rune.

Moonlight's a hidden promise
the silvered path on a loch
the space in a hidden corner
the secret inside a box.

Moonlight's a haunted vessel
a ghost in an empty tomb
a light to guide the angels
a face in a darkened room.

Moonlight's a shade for dreaming
the billowing cloak of the wind
the misty souls of black rivers
the glitter on midnight's wings.

A QUESTION OF A SNAKE

King
Cobra in your
black and gold. But is your
heart so ssstony cold? Or do
you cry, what evil ssscore
dubbed yooou, uncaring
carnivore? When you
kisss your victim's
neck, do tearsss
fall in sssad
regret,
that
your
only
form
of greeting,
is taste to sssee
if it's worth eating? Help
Asss you dance you
ssspread your hood.
Do you feeeeeeeel
misunderstood,
when quarry
frozen
ssstiff
with
fear,
feeelss
death'ss
the one
caresss   you share?
Slipping   sssoftly   into
sssleep,   do you   ponder
those   you eat?   What
venom   is it that   you
own, living   hated

alone?

and

81

METAPHOR

I'm the flame in the nettle's sting
the fleet snow of goose's wing.
I'm the feather in grass's seed
wheaten waves in meadow's sea.

I'm the bamboo legs of cranes
the dandelion's ochre mane.
I'm the spider's gossamer thread
the ivory pea in oyster's bed.

I'm the river's diamond sheen
the whispering of forest's green.
I'm hell's gate in thunder's cloud
stiff petticoats on blossom's robe.

I'm the pipes that play the wind
the silvered song moonbeams sing.
I'm the petal fists of butterflies
angel footprints across dark skies.

I'm the nightmare's cloven feet
the candy stripes of puffin's beak.
I'm the cook that stirs the storm
the softened face of rising dawn.

I'm the sandman's daylight dream
the looking glass of what may seem
painting pictures, palettes of words
reaping the treasures of the world.

ARACHINE

On a silken castle she rests her sceptre
of chipped armour, reluctant suitors.

She weaves a shroud for the funeral party,
letting down tresses, spinning out circles

on webbed mirrors of looted brambles
in her shed stockade thistledown city.

Gourds of wasp paper, flaked lead crystal,
orbs of black beetles, bluebottle bangles,

a long summer cloak of butterfly petals,
ladybird bowls for her banqueting table,

sailing the breeze of grizzle-drunk bees,
each drop fizzing down stairs of husk,

lost in the veils of her poisoned mantle,
the taste of tomb in her venom cups.

Death descends on a gossamer thread,
pearl, aphid-crowned, neck-laced in ants.

Caressing them stiffly she weaves a net
and taking her needle stitches them up.

JACK

When Jack wakes, he oozes chill
and from his cloak of frosted silk
pours glitters for the limbs of trees
shrouds their leaves in winter's milk.

He sends out shards into the lake
paints the glass with sugared lace
and crisps the grass with frosty feet
then burns the winter sun with ice.

He doffs a cap of driven sleet
shivers snowflakes from his hair
then wanders down the crystal road
and leaves diamonds everywhere.

MISS MOON

Late,
when the
garden's
lit soft grey,
only Miss
Moon in
the idle dark,
shifts in the
restless apple
tree, combing
her mane of
cloudy stars. I
feel her silver eyes
upon me, see
moonlight
shriven on the
wall, waxing,
her bright
smile so
enchanted,
I promise
her the
sleeping
world.

MOTORWAY POEM

after *Night Mail* by WH Auden

These are the bright motorway hoardings
above the dead fox and pigeon corpses.

Clouds rushing past, cars starting to flow,
a man in a Porsche shouts into his phone.

Signs for McDonald's, roadside cafés,
the lights are on red, it's taking all day.

Past wide-loads that are straddling lanes
and the constant threat of a possible delay.

Major roadworks, what a din,
Costa Coffee and Burger King.

Speed cameras that cause congestion,
car windows with the sky's reflection.

White campervan, Live Aquatics,
Steve Wright on the radio, playing classics.

Patchwork fields of mustard seeds,
sprouting hedges and lacy trees.

A nodding dog looks up, surprised,
trainers and a doll, left where they lie.

Chopping and changing, picking up speed,
a little boy waving from a booster seat.

No hard shoulder for half a mile,
traffic cones in single file.

Down towards Birmingham, starting to slow,
four miles an hour and still far to go.

End of the motorway, we're sitting pretty,
lorries and cars bleed into the city.

Down busy streets, under high-rise blocks,
past restaurants and chaotic shops,

grocers and banks, parking convoys,
sweaters and pants, windows of toys,

people meeting with salutations
and couples hugging in light flirtations

and people asking for cash donations,
new developments and late embellishments,

houses with backyards and tiny gardens,
houses with murals and billboard bargains,

houses with railings and wheelchair ramps,
houses with shutters and wild climbing plants,

the shadow of a church's steeple,
Public Houses full of people.

Students queuing for the next big thing,
some with tattoos or a nasal ring,

in trainers and jeans, covered in bling,
the natty, the batty, the warring, the imploring,

those with a home here, those that are boarding.
Alleys with trolleys, wheels long gone,

the graffiti on the viaduct where the paint has run,
babies in buggies fast asleep,

sisters, brothers, teens and toddlers,
crying for sweets and chips and burgers

or iced buns from the local bakers.
Outside the car-park men are working,

outside the hotel a new diversion,
away from the exit and the entrance.

We try again
but it's no better

and horns sound if
we slow or stop.

So near and yet
so hard to find when you keep being driven round the block.

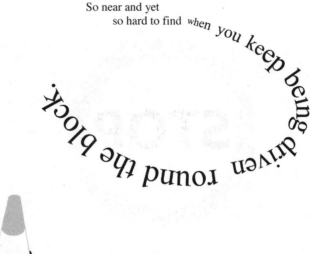

THE KISS

I found an autumn necklace in the hedge,
silken threads, strung with tiny beads.
Yet when I touched a strand it fell,
leaving only scattered tears.

I found a winter diamond on the wall,
cold and sharp as dragon's scale.
Yet though I locked it in a box,
somehow it stole itself away.

I found spring dancers in the wood,
their faces reaching for the sun.
Yet when I put them in a glass
each grew heavy on its stem.

I found a summer moon beside the road,
floating in a shallow pool.
Yet as I lifted it, it broke.
I cried: I'd meant to let it go.

Mum wrapped me in her strong warm arms,
showed me the moon, still small and new.
Some things, she said, *cannot be owned,*
then gave me a kiss. I have it still.

ACKNOWLEDGEMENTS

The following poems were previously published in anthologies as listed below:

A Question of a Snake – *Masala, Poems from India, Bangladesh, Pakistan and Sri Lanka*, chosen by Debjani Chatterjee, published by Macmillan Children's Books, 2005

The Frog Princess and Terrible Lizards – *Shouting at the Ocean*, chosen by Graham Denton, Andrea Shavick and Roger Stevens, published by Hands Up Books, 2009

Holiday Blues and Poem About the Injustice of Being Made to Stand Outside in the Rain at Playtime – *Read Me at School*, chosen by Gaby Morgan, published by Macmillan Children's Books, 2009

The Kiss – *A Time to Speak and A Time to Listen*, chosen by Celia Warren, published by Schofield and Sims, 2013

Old Dog – *Puppy Poems*, chosen by Gaby Morgan and Jane Eccles, published by Macmillan Children's Books, 2011

Old Foxy – *The RSPB Anthology of Wildlife Poems*, chosen by Celia Warren, published by Bloomsbury Children's Books, 2012

Planet for Sale – *Let's Recycle Grandad*, chosen by Roger Stevens, published by A & C Black, 2008

The Poe Tree (a version of) – *Let's Celebrate*, chosen by Debjani Chatterjee and Brian D'Arcy, published by Frances Lincoln Children's Books, 2011

Talking Toads – *Teaching Pack for Larkin with Toads Project, Hull,* 2012

Where Zebras Go – *Let in the Stars, New Poetry for Children,* chosen by Leone Anabella Betts, Carole Bromley and Mandy Coe, published by Manchester Metropolitan University, 2014

SUE HARDY-DAWSON

is a Yorkshire-born poet, artist and illustrator who has
been widely published in children's poetry anthologies.
Before becoming a poet she worked with children for
over twenty years. In 2014 she was Highly Commended
for the Manchester Writing for Children Prize.
She has an Open First Class Honours Degree in
Creative Writing, Literature and Supporting Teaching
and Learning from the Open University. When not
writing or drawing, she likes to visit schools and has
also been commissioned to provide workshops for
the Prince of Wales Foundation for Children and the
Arts. She is dyslexic and takes a special interest in
encouraging reluctant readers and writers.
Where Zebras Go is Sue Hardy-Dawson's debut
solo collection. She lives with her family
in Harrogate, Yorkshire.